"Beyond 2"

Tales From Life...
Strange But True

Edited By

Marilyn Wright Dayton

Beyond 2

Copyright © 2021 Marilyn Wright Dayton

ISBN: # 9798595509749

DEDICATION

I would like to dedicate this book to all those who have unusual stories to tell but may find it difficult to share them. Sometimes we believe that we need to keep some stories to ourselves, because to tell you the truth, who would believe them??

So, to those who have contributed to this book, who have relived some sort of scary or strange experience by telling their story or stories to us, I thank you. I know how difficult it was. And, no, I don't believe that you are a bit mad or crazy. Because then, I would be too, as some of these stories are my own experiences. And I get goose bumps just reliving/remembering them, because they really are a bit strange, a bit 'out there', even though I know that they are true. I saw them. I lived them. I remember them, just as if they had happened yesterday.

Marilyn
AUTHOR

CONTENTS

Beyond 2

PREFACE

These are real stories, from real people. They may be a bit strange but are true. You may read them and have doubts. We are sharing them with you in the hope that you at least will enjoy them, even through any doubts you may feel.

Ralph Waldo Emerson said,
> *" The purpose of life is not to be happy. It is to be useful, to be honorable, to be compassionate, to have it make some difference that you lived and lived well."*

Part of living in this world is to try to make that difference. What if we still have work to do in order to have lived better? Are we completely gone after we die? We may never know the answer to that. Perhaps some of the 'spirits' in these stories want to still share their 'space' or share their stories with us.

Sharing our life experiences sometimes brings a level of satisfaction to our lives, with the hopes that we are entertaining others. No matter what the subject is. These stories may seem a bit strange to you. But, for those of us who have experienced them, they can be strange, but for us, they are true. We, each of us who have contributed to this book, hope that you read each tale with an open mind.

To that end, thank you for respecting that we are all different and have lived different lives from one another. And we all have stories to tell, some a bit difficult to tell. That is why our story contributors/authors wish to remain anonymous, with us showing you only our initials and where we live.

Beyond 2

"The Old Inn"
- Sometimes we are in the wrong place at the right time. –

 I was having a night out with a couple of girl friends to try to catch up with one another's lives. We met at a very old inn in their tavern. We were talking with the bartender about how old the inn was, and he said it had been around since the late 18th Century. The tavern was charming, with a lot of wood beams, and a very comfortable feeling to it. We wondered about the other parts of the inn, and he offered to get the manager to give us a little tour of some of the rooms. He added that some of them *"held a surprise."* Not clarifying what he meant, he went off in search of the manager.

 She was very nice about giving us a little tour, but we could only see a few rooms as the other rooms were occupied by guests. We stopped just outside one of the rooms, which she had saved for last, *"This one is the most interesting. The room itself is quite plain, we left it as it looked originally as best as we could. This room was Abigail's room when she was a young lady. She was quite young still when she died. And to this day she visits her room, so you may see some signs of her. Feel free to take a look."* And she stepped aside so we could enter.

Even though the room was simple, it was charming. Her bedspread looked quite old, but in good condition. There were some pictures that were supposed to be hung on one wall but had been left propped against the wall on the floor. When we went back out into the hallway, the manager explained, *"Yes, she does that all the time. We hang them back up, and she takes them down. We really don't know why. But it does make for an interesting story, doesn't it?"* She asked us to wait while she went in and hung the pictures back up on the wall. When she returned, she suggested we wait for a few minutes and then go back into the room and see if they had been removed again. After just a few minutes when she was telling us a little more about the inn's history, we decided to check out the room again.

The three of us stepped into the room, and as we looked towards the wall on our right, we saw that the pictures had again been neatly placed on the floor, propped up against the wall. And this time, the bedspread had been folded differently, as if Abigail had made the bed ready for sleeping. The sheet and covers were folded very neatly down along the bed about a foot lower than the pillows. And the room felt quite chilly.

We went back out and told the manager about the bedspread change, and she frowned, *"That's strange. She doesn't usually do that. Perhaps she was inviting one of you to spend the night in her room."* She smiled and said, *"You would be surprised by what we see here sometimes. Some of our guests tell us about people in period clothes walking up and down the hallway as if searching for something. I have been told that Abigail was quite a pretty little thing, although I haven't seen her myself.*" Then we all walked back down the hallway toward the door that would lead us back into the tavern.

I asked the manager, "*Aren't you going to fix her room back the way it was?*" And she smiled and said, "*Why I don't think so. I will leave it like that for awhile. When Abigail feels like there will be no one coming into the room again for a while, she might let our changes stay for a few days.*" And the manager walked away, leaving us wishing we could have met that pretty young spirit. Perhaps another time. But we were definitely ready for a strong drink after that experience. It was rather unnerving to say the least.

-    *From M.D. from Connecticut*

"The Sweet Shoppe and the Wedding"

- We all have heard about strange happenings that become stories we hear from friends or family. -

The sweet shoppe, a sort of Mom-Pop grocery store was on North Queen Street, across from my aunt's house. There were twin brothers, both in the Navy, who were my mother's cousins. We will call them Josh and John. John was home on leave, preparing for his wedding. The last time that Josh was on leave, he had promised John that he would be back in time for his brother's wedding to serve as best man. This was something that they had agreed all of their lives, that they would be there for each other's wedding. Josh was still overseas but had promised he would be there for the wedding.

The day before the wedding, they still hadn't heard from him, and John was getting concerned. Then they received a telegram that day from Josh saying that he was on his way and would be home to be in the wedding. The next morning, they were preparing for the wedding. They planned to stop at the shoppe to pick up some goodies for the wedding. In those days, the shops were different in Ireland. You would see some of their wares in a window, but you had to go along the alleyway to the back where there was an entry door, and that's how you went into the shoppe. It wasn't necessarily a store front like today.

Anyway, so John was on his way over to the shoppe, and who came along on the other side of the street but Josh, and John saw him and yelled over, *"Josh, you made it!"* Josh waved back at him and yelled over *"I told you I would be here for your wedding. I'll see you at home."* So, while Josh headed to the house, John went to the shoppe. When John returned from the shoppe to the house to get ready to go to the church, he asked his mother if Josh had arrived yet, and his mother didn't know what he was talking about. John told her that Josh was here, home in time for the wedding, and that he had been heading over to their house. As they were talking about it, there arrived a couple of representatives of the Navy to tell them that Josh had been killed in action. He was killed just before he was able to leave to come home. And, of course, John couldn't believe it, as he had just seen his brother walking down the street and had spoken to him.

So it ended up that he had *'made it home for the wedding as promised'* but had actually died before he could physically come home. I was too young to witness this, but I remember the shoppe, and heard this story many times from my family.

-   *From P.S. from Connecticut*

"Playing the Piano"

- Sometimes we don't realize that we have an audience from 'someplace else'... –

I grew up loving music. Both of my parents are musicians and teach it. Apparently, I even hum songs in my sleep, according to my husband. We were on vacation, visiting a cousin in the UK. She lives in one of these very old castle-type homes, which has been renovated and updated mostly, but once in awhile on a windy day, you can feel a draft. Anyway, they have a music room with a beautiful, old grand piano. I couldn't wait to play it. Everyone was out that day, having gone to see a football/soccer game, not something I have any interest in. I figured this was to be the day when I could sit down and play some music, alone in my enjoyment.

I always have felt that it was a wondrous feeling when I was alone, caught up in my music. I finished one of the harder pieces that I know well, and as I was sitting back, reveling how I remembered the piece which I hadn't played in a long time, a piece written by Beethoven. Suddenly, I heard clapping coming from behind me in this huge room. It was echoing off the walls. I felt myself blush, and turned around to thank the person, whoever it was. And no one was there. I called out *"Hello?"* Then I rose and walked out of the room, looking down the long hallway, and saw no one. It felt a bit creepy.

When everyone returned from the game, all revved up and talking at once, I pulled my cousin aside and asked him who else had stayed in the house. He told me they had all been gone, even the servants who had the afternoon off. When I told him that someone had been there and clapped after I played a Beethoven piece, he laughed, *"Oh, that is just Hattie. She lived here over a hundred years ago and loved music. You can hear her humming every once in a while. And she loved Beethoven."* And he walked away. Uh...what????

\-   *From C.L. of California*

"The Security Guard"

-Protecting our children is so important. And sometimes we find that others are watching over them too.-

This was my experience when my three boys were young. I had a big pram so that the three of them could sit in it. But, my elder boy would hold onto the pram, while the little ones were in the pram.

I used to walk everywhere, and so was on my way to the bank on West Chester Avenue. Before I went into the bank, I parked the pram (in those days, it was safe to leave your baby outside by the door while you did your business inside, if it didn't take too long.) So, I parked it, and this man came over to me. He was older, wore a navy color security uniform, gold trim, with the badge of the bank on it. My two older boys were standing beside me, holding my hand, and the baby was asleep in the pram.

The man greeted me and offered to watch over the baby while I went into the bank. He was so pleasant, and since he wore the bank security guard uniform, I figured that it would be OK. He walked over and put his hand on my older boy's head and said *"This child is going to go places; he is going to make a name for himself when he gets older. He will have a good life, with of course ups and downs, but he will have a good life and you will be proud of him."* That was so nice of him to say, and I told him so, thanking him. He shook my other son's hand and said hello to him. He then said he would watch over the baby while I took the older two boys into the bank with me. He said to me, *"You have a good life now."* I thanked him again. Before I went inside, he reminded me to remember what he said. Then I turned and we went into the bank.

I came back out again, and the man was nowhere around. I had only been gone for about five minutes, and the pram and baby were now alone. One of the girls from the bank had followed me out as she was going to lunch. She asked me what the matter was, and I told her that I was wondering where the man had gone. I described him to her and she said there was no need for guards at their bank so no security guards worked there. I told her the story and described him to her. She took me back into the bank to talk with the manager, who confirmed that there was no security guard there. I told him that I spent more time talking with the man than I spent inside the bank and was sure that he worked for them. Again, no one worked as a security guard for them.

I didn't find out until later on that there was this girl that used to work for them, and her father used to come and meet her in front of the bank. He had been a security guard, but for another place. He used to wait until she was done at work and he used to walk her home. While he waited, he used to talk with everyone he met outside the bank, being a very nice man. And he had died about six years earlier.

-    *From P.S. from Connecticut*

"Haunting on Block Island"

-Spirits can be all around us, waiting for 'us to visit'.-

It was the summer of 2016, and my husband and I decided to enjoy a long weekend on Block Island, RI. Having been before, we always enjoyed the beautiful views, ocean breezes and entertainment. I recall booking a hotel room, sight unseen. in anticipation for the weekend.

We departed the ferry and took a quick cab ride to the hotel. From the moment we arrived, I could feel a palpable energy surrounding the building. It felt as if it had the lives of its predecessors attached to it.

With slight trepidation, my husband and I approached the hotel. It was indeed quaint, sitting atop a hill, overlooking New Harbor in all its beauty. On a warm August day, with few clouds, the island was in all its splendor. We took the steps to the second floor and I began to feel a ghost-like presence strengthen in the hallway.

Having been sensitive to the presence of spirits since I was a child, it was clear to me this place was indeed haunted!

We began to unpack with the door to the hotel room open. Seconds upon beginning to unpack, I heard a creak in the hallway. I looked up and saw a tall, slender man, over six feet, in his late thirties with wavy dark hair to the length of his neckline. He was dressed in a navy blue captain's uniform that looked of the time era of mid to late 1800's. Intent on his purpose, he walked by our room, out to the balcony...and then disappeared into thin air!

With a racing heart. I exclaimed to my husband "*Did you see that ghost?*" With a bit of skepticism, he said that he had not. We went about our day, and later returned to the hotel to see the stunning sunset.

We enjoyed a drink while viewing the magnificent sunset. Out of the corner of my eye, I saw the same man, walking around the outside of the hotel building. Our server, who had worked at the hotel for several years was very amicable. I started speaking with her, and I asked: "*Is this hotel haunted?*" She tossed her head back, erupted in a tense laugh.

"*Oh yes, it's haunted. There've been a few spirits that have made their way through here over the years. The various help that have stayed in the Carriage House, two of the innkeepers, and even a couple of frequent guests have seen them.*" I described what I had seen, and she exclaimed that it was the original innkeeper, who had been a former naval captain. Talk about validation!

● ● ●

We went to sleep later that evening, somewhat fitful on my part. My husband, an early riser, awoke at 6:00. He looked outside the window, and through the morning mist, saw the very same spirit that I had. I knew it was accurate, as his description matched mine spot on.

I can only guess that the same spirits are active there. Though I'm not entirely sure I'll go back to find out. Time will tell...

-    *From H.P. from Connecticut*

"Whispers In My Ear"

- We all have that ability to feel as if someone we love is in trouble or that we need to contact them. –

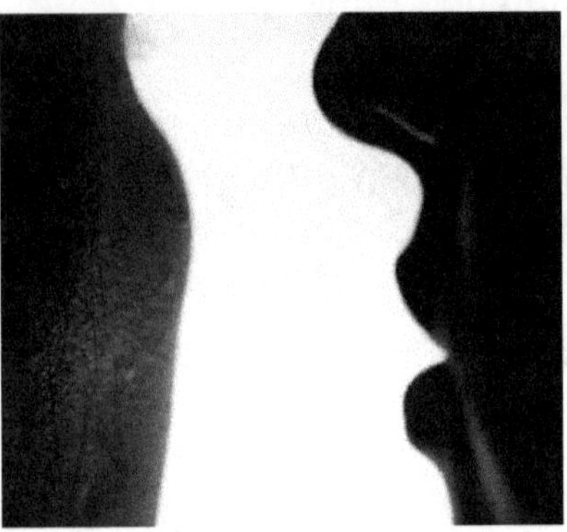

My brother (my only sibling) and I were close all of our lives. He was a great older brother, watching over me, teaching me things, and protecting me from bullies in school. I had been a shy kid, so I was fodder for any bully, since I didn't say much, and lowered my head when confronted. (I definitely outgrew that and am quite an extrovert now.)

At any rate, by the time we were adults, each with our own families, living about 1,000 miles apart, we did keep in touch with letters and phone calls a few times a year. And each time, it was as if we had been together just the day before, it was so comfortable. We would be silly, crack jokes, while we got caught up with each other's lives.

I was in my home office, working on something for my small business that I ran from home, when I began to feel uncomfortable. I couldn't figure out what was wrong with me. One thing I knew was that something had happened to someone I cared about. I just didn't know who or what. It stayed with me the rest of the day and night.

The next morning, I decided to begin making phone calls to see if everyone in my family was ok. When I was deciding who to call first, I thought I heard someone whispering in my ear to call my brother. I looked around, but no one was there. But I got a rather "creepy" feeling, so I figured all right, I will. And he answered right away, saying *"How did you know?"* Then adding, *"Oh, yeah, I forgot, you are very intuitive and would have some sort of premonition about what happened."* This was something that happened with me quite often...call it women's intuition or being very sensitive to what is happening to people *'in my universe'*. It always proved right when I felt it. But this time, I had heard a whisper that helped distract me from the work I was doing. And I am grateful.

I asked him, *"What happened? Are you okay?"*

He said, *"Sure, I'm okay now. But I wasn't yesterday afternoon around 2 or so."* (That was when I got that strange feeling. Although it was actually 3 in my time zone.) So I asked him to tell me about it.

"Well, I was working up on the roof, and when I went to step onto the ladder to come down, I missed the step and fell off the roof."

I could feel myself holding my breath. *"Did you get hurt?"*

"Well, yeah, a little. I fell on top of the car. Even dented the roof on it a little." I was holding my breath again.

"Margie was the only one home (his daughter), and she was in her bedroom listening to music so she didn't hear

anything. So, when I woke up around an hour or two later, still laying on top of the car, I thought I should probably check and see if anything was broken." Again holding my breath, after taking a quick gasp.

"Yeah, my leg hurt quite a bit, but it seemed to function okay, just felt badly bruised. So I came inside and put some ice on it to help the swelling that was happening and to keep the bruise from getting too bad."

After taking a deep breath, I made some additional suggestions, such as getting himself checked out by a doctor in case there was something he had done that he didn't know about. He promised to do that, that he would call the doctor right after we hung up. It had already been almost 24 hours, but he was *'such a man'* about things like that. So, I asked him to let me know how he was in a few days, unless they find something that was wrong first.

About a week later, I called him (of course) and he said he was doing okay, but they were concerned about a blood clot in his leg, hoping that it would dissolve soon. After telling him that he *"was a damn fool for not having someone around while he climbed on top of the house,"* we ended the call with love and hugs.

I didn't hear from him again until my birthday a couple of months later. He always called me on my birthday to sing to me and make me laugh. After that, all seemed well, and he and his family moved back East. Exactly a year and ineteen days later, he died, after going for a jog where he felt something wrong with his same leg and had called the doctor *'like a good boy'*. He had been on his way out the door to go to the doctor and suffered a pulmonary embolism which immediately killed him. It was a blood clot from his leg that had been injured. He was not even 58 years young.

I am grateful for whoever whispered in my ear that day, and so glad I got to talk with him. It is difficult to stay in touch when you grow up and go your separate ways. I am glad we worked at not letting too much time go by without talking. But he died too soon. It has been 20 years since this happened, and I miss him every day.

-   *From M.D. from Connecticut*

"The Empty Swing"

- It can happen to anyone. One minute you are walking through a park, the next something is happening. Something weird. –

There was a small playground near our home when I was a preteen. A curious thing happened there, and it still stays in my mind these forty years later. I had been told that there was one swing we couldn't touch because it *'was haunted'*. Sure. But of course, I didn't touch it.

One morning I was passing through there, earlier than I usually do. And I saw *'that swing'* in full motion, going back and forth, not slowing down. I stood there, trying to figure out how it was doing that. After a few minutes, as I was about to walk away, the swing slowed down. I could hear a child's laugh, faint but clear. And then the swing stopped. I felt goosebumps on my body and ran off. I didn't think about it until the next day, same time, same place. Yup, it was swinging again. Then it slowed down and I heard the child's laugh again.

I just couldn't stand there any longer and be near that place where the '*ghost child*' was. I had trouble sleeping for awhile. One day I was talking with a neighbor and told him about the swing and what I saw and heard. He told me the story, which was so sad. There had been a little boy about 5 who lived nearby who loved the swings. He picked that particular swing and went to the playground every morning at the same early time, usually alone but sometimes with his older brother. And he enjoyed the swing for a while until he had to go back home. And he laughed as he got off the swing. One day a car swerved and hit the boy as he was going back home. He loved swinging so much that every day at the same time in the early morning, he (or his ghost) comes there enjoying himself and laughing.

Most people avoid the playground around that time of the morning, due to being very uncomfortable with the thought of a ghost. I can understand that, as I never went there again. And we moved away a short time later and I tried to forget about it. But every once in a while when I hear a child laugh, I think of it. And I always get goosebumps and feel both sad and a bit scared to tell the truth.

- *By T. D. from Georgia*

"Ghost at the Museum"

-Sometimes we are the only ones 'to see'.-

It was 2007. I was living on my own. I had recently reconnected with a man from my past after a five-year hiatus. We had run in the same circles and had been friends. The week earlier, he had asked me on a date. For whatever reason, I obliged, thinking it would go nowhere. We met in the Stonington Borough for our first date. We went on a beautiful boat ride overlooking Stonington Harbor and Watch Hill. Afterward, we went for a walk around the Borough, learning about one another.

We walked through to the end of the Borough, which is a peninsula that overlooks Watch Hill, Barn Island and Fishers Island. We walked down to the east side of what is called "*The Point*" and sat on a stone bench. To the back is the Lighthouse Museum, a museum that holds much history in the Borough.

I took a glimpse behind me to watch the sunset as it was a gorgeous late summer evening. As I turned to look behind me, I saw an older woman gazing at us. Her bun tight, her eyes kind and softly staring, just to the back door of the Museum.

"Do you see the woman looking at us? Who is she? Do you know her?" I said to my date. He turned to look at me as I asked him, then looked at the door as I was continuing to watch her. *"I don't see anyone,"* he chuckled. *"Are you seeing things?"*

At the risk of seeming awkward, I let out a soft *"Well, maybe."* I then watched the woman go down the stairs and walk around outside in the front of the building. With each step, her presence and form literally disappeared with each step. It was all a bit scary.

One thing that I will never forget is the surprising sense of peace and kindness that I had felt from her.

This first date turned out to become my husband. I'm not sure if the ghost I saw was looking towards us knowing and hopeful for the future. However, I do know she taught me that there are spirits that can look after us with kindness.

- *From H.P. of Connecticut*

"The Little Girl"

-Finding that we are 'not alone' can be eerie.-

We lived in Florida at the time. We had a pool outside, as many do there because of the heat. So, one day I was sitting watching television, and I looked up and saw a little girl standing in front of my door that led out to the pool. She was maybe around five years old or so, wearing a little swim outfit, pink and cute. She had shoulder length blond hair, and just stood there looking at me. I didn't know who she was or how she had gotten inside my house. She was only there for a little bit, then she was gone. She just went *"poof"* and disappeared. I had no idea who she was, having no idea about the history of the house I lived in.

A day or so later, I talked with one of my neighbors across the street, an older couple. I asked them if they knew who the little girl could have been and if she had died there.

They couldn't remember specifically, but thought they remembered someone who had lived there with little children. Something apparently happened there, and they had moved away shortly afterwards. Could be the little girl drowned, but they weren't sure.

And strange but, the man died a couple of days later. I had a strange feeling that they knew more than they were saying to me, that perhaps they had known the family more than they indicated, perhaps even being related. It was just a strange feeling about it. And I only saw her once. Did she want me to talk to the man before he died? I really don't know, it was just a one-time thing. But it was a bit strange.

-    *From P.S. in Connecticut*

"The Elevator"

-Seeing someone 'from there' can feel weird.-

My family and I were in France for vacation. We rented a suite in a gorgeous old inn, being fortunate enough to find one on the top floor. There were only five floors, but the building made up for rustic atmosphere and great views on that floor. I think that if there were more floors, it wouldn't have been as special.

Anyway, we always took the elevator up and down, as my father couldn't do stairs very well, having a bit of a heart condition. This was the last vacation we took before he passed away, the following Winter. Our parents had gone to a museum and being teenagers, my brother and myself decided to change and go for a hike in the town. This was Provence, a gorgeous part of the country, with wine villas and fields, and more nature than people. We waited for the one elevator that they had, ready to board it when a young man stepped beside us. He was dressed funny, perhaps he was an actor in costume was what we thought.

Anyway, when the elevator arrived, he walked ahead

● ● ●

of us, turned around and held his hand up to stop us from getting in. We looked at each other, wondering what was going on. He bowed, smiled, and the door closed. The elevator went up to the fifth floor, stopped and came back down.

But we were too curious and decided to ask the person at the front desk about him. Speaking very little English, but enough to get through, he explained that it was *"Guillaume"* who had lived there about a hundred years before. The sad part was that he had fallen down the elevator shaft (the shaft had been left open and not completed with the new elevator 'machine'). Over the years, he liked to travel in the elevator, but always alone. He would warn others not to get in with him, they think to keep others safe. He told us we were lucky to witness the vision, as only special *"sensitive"* people could see him so clearly.

We were quite spooked and couldn't wait to leave a few days later, being quite nervous every time we went to that elevator. Actually the whole thing spooked us out so much, we hardly slept the rest of the time we were there. We thought maybe he would come in our room or something. We were only in our early teens, generally quite independent, but our imaginations were going wild after that experience.

We were happy to go home. Afterwards, we had wished we had taken his picture with our cameras (before iPhones), to see if it would have shown him or if it would have been nothing that showed up. When I think of it today, some 30 years later, I get goosebumps. One *'vision'* like that is enough in a lifetime.

-   *From T. W. from England*

"The Scotland B&B"

-When you travel to either the European Continent or the Island of Great Britain, you need to be aware that their countries are old, filled with old 'memories'.-

My late husband and I used to love to travel when we could. We would usually go to the Southwestern US to see the gorgeous red cliffs of Zion National Park or the Sedona area, one of our favorite spots. This time, we headed out of the country to visit with friends in London, England. We wanted to see Wimbledon where we could see some of our favorite tennis pros play. Very exciting for me, being a huge tennis fan.

One day we decided to travel by train to Edinburgh and see the streets of the old city and witness the International Festival that was being held. We decided to stay at a Bed & Breakfast and found a very quaint but beautiful one within walking distance to the castle. We were excited as there was so much to see, and we asked our hostess about some suggestions of things we could see and do. She gave us a few ideas and a couple of brochures, then smiling, she told us about our accommodations.

"The room you will be staying in was Mary's room. She visits us often and you might see her at night, most probably in the hallway after dark." We look at each other, not understanding. I asked her, *"If we are in her room, then where will she stay?"*

"Oh, I am so sorry, I wasn't clear. You see, Mary lived here a long time ago. She still visits us often, even after over 200 years, even plays a tune on the piano sometimes. She plays beautifully."

My husband and I looked at each other, his eyes rolling in mock of her, but mine were large and curious. I love ghosts and would love to see her. So I asked her, *"Will Mary mind us being in her room?"*

Our hostess smiled and said, *"If you don't actually get to see her, she will show how she feels about you in some fashion. You will know it when it happens."* And she left it at that.

We decided to drop off our luggage in the room and freshen up quickly as we were anxious to start strolling the old streets and see what the town looks like up close. So, I went into the attached bathroom we were lucky to have, and washed up quickly, returning to see my husband engrossed in our tour book. Then, I noticed that the bed had been turned down for us. *"Oh, how nice. When did our hostess come in and turn down the bed?"* He looked up, shrugged and said, *"No one came in."*

I knew that our bed had not been turned down when we came in. So, curious, I went over and tucked the covers back in under the pillows. He went into the bathroom, while I picked up the tour book and sat down to take a look. When he came back out into the room, I looked up, noticing that the bed covers had been turned down again. Also, a photo from the wall had suddenly gone missing. Glancing around the room, I noticed a part of the picture frame sticking out from behind the bedside table. Smiling, I looked towards the bed and said, *"It's OK Mary. I didn't think that picture was very pretty either."*

My husband frowned at me but didn't say anything. As we were leaving the room, I looked back saying, *"Thank you, Mary for welcoming us to your room."*

As we walked down the hallway anxious to start our adventure, I turned to my husband and said, *"I do so hope that we get to actually see Mary before we leave here."* He just scowled at me, making a *"Hmmph"* sound. Anything that couldn't be explained wasn't his kind of thing. But it was definitely mine. We never did get to actually see Mary, sad to say. Although she did turn down our bed covers the following night for us.

-   *From M.D. from Connecticut*

"Just Passing Through"

-Another visitor in the night.-

In 1990, I was twelve years old, soon to be thirteen. While young, I was reasonably mature for my age. I was in my childhood home on Old Mystic. It was a full moon, and an unseasonably cold night.

Perhaps it was the full moon, perhaps it was the cold, but that night of sleep was restless. I awoke at one point with the light of the moon streaming through my window, aghast at what I was seeing.

A middle-aged man, in a trench coat and fedora was standing to my left. He was just shy of six feet tall. Frozen, I closed my eyes and reopened them. Had I been dreaming? Alas, I was not, as he was still there. Through what I can only describe as mental telepathy, he began to speak.

* * *

Beyond 2

"Please do not be scared. I used to live here, and I'm just passing through for a visit. Everything is OK." I remained in the same position, and yet, after his words, felt an odd sense of calm. He remained for about another 30 seconds, though it felt like a year. And then disappeared into the moonlight as he walked away.

Oddly, I fell asleep with a different kind of calm. An insight, so to speak and at my young age, an interesting take on the lives before us. A life from the past, just passing through.

-   *From H.P. from Connecticut*

"The House on Jameson Street"

-It can take someone a while before they 'cross over' because they still have a job to do.-

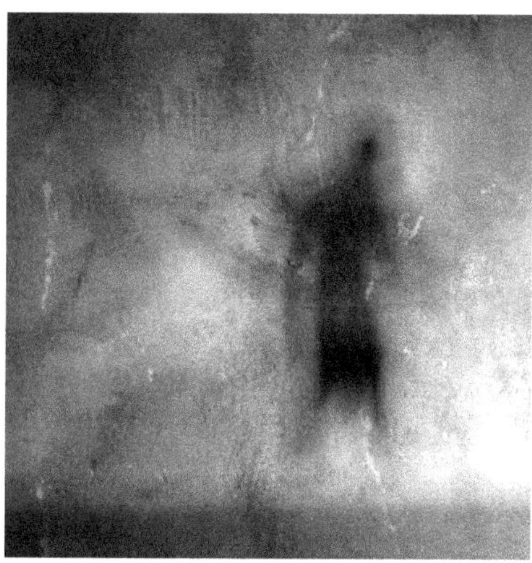

There are two stories here,happening the same night. Back in Ireland, it seemed like almost everyone had two chairs by the fireplace, one being a red chair specifically. And we were living there for a short time, not quite a year, when my second husband had a job setting up a restaurant there. Anyway, I was sitting there watching a program on the television that I became quite engrossed in. My ten-year-old son was asleep in a little bedroom upstairs, he had school the next day.

I suddenly felt a hand coming along my neck. My first husband used to rub my neck a lot. I was so engrossed in the show that I swatted the air saying *"Will you stop it Patrick, get away from me."* (That was my first husband's name.) I told him I wanted to see the show. He did it again, with the hand coming around my neck, then down my arm and back up again. Now I was paying attention, as I felt this coldness, as if he had then sat on the arm of the chair next to me. And I realized what had happened, that I recognized who he was.

At that moment, my son called out to me in his sleep. So, I went running up the stairs, and stopped in my tracks, as there was a woman standing at the top of the stairs. The bathroom was right there and she had walked out of the bathroom, and then she walked into my son's room. I asked her *"What are you doing?"* as I ran into his room. I found him sitting up in the bed, and I asked him what the matter was, and he responded, *"I don't know."* I asked him why he was shouting, and he didn't remember doing that. He told me that something had woken him up. Then he laid back down, turned onto his side and went right back to sleep.

Meanwhile, the lady had left his room, going back into the bathroom. After I left my son's room, I went to go back down the stairs, and I felt this coldness. The lady was behind me at the bathroom door. I didn't know who she was. She was an older lady, pretty white hair up into a bun at the back of her head, wearing this long white dress with little maroon flowers on it, with lacy collar and sleeves, and wearing an apron. And she wore a sweater around her shoulders. She wore glasses and pearl earrings. She proceeded to head back into my son's room.

I sat on the stair and waited, and watched her repeat this action several times, from the bathroom to the bedroom, back to the bathroom, only to repeat the action. She never acknowledged me, didn't even seem to see me. This happened every night.

A few days later, I mentioned this to my mother, and asked her if she knew who this could be. She was a doubter, but she did agree to talk with my landlord when he came over for his rent. She suggested I ask him, but I wasn't able to get there in time when he came over. I wondered if someone died in that house. She did ask him about the day, and he said that it was his mother that had owned the house. She didn't ask him if the lady had died there, as she didn't believe in spirits or ghosts and just sluffed that part off. So I let it go.

The visits of this lady went on for almost the year that we lived there. Also from time to time, my first husband's spirit would visit, just to touch me with his hand on my cheek or neck. I got used to it all, what else could I do? The last week we were there, we were packing, and had to sign paperwork with the landlord. So, he came to our house and I was able to ask him. I described her to him, and he told me the story.

He showed me a picture of her, and it was the lady. It was his mother. She had been taking care of his father who was ill for several years. She had him in the same bedroom where my son was. She used to go from the bathroom with cold cloths into the bedroom to tend to his father. He asked me if she talked to me at all, and I told him no. And funny, he gave me back a deposit that I had never given to him because I didn't talk to others about the experience. And he asked me to say a prayer for her.

-   *From P.S. in Connecticut*

"Premonition of a Disaster

-She needed to get on that plane. Why was everything going wrong?-

I know this has sometimes happened to other people, a premonition that could be disastrous. Sometimes it is a misunderstanding that leads them to miss an event, where they would have been killed. Sometimes it is a car accident that keeps them from arriving at a scene where a disaster occurs. For me, it was one of my children having a meltdown that kept me from catching my plane.

I was scheduled to attend a conference for work. I really wasn't looking forward to it because I hated going out of town for any length of time that kept me from being with my family. My youngest was particularly angry this one morning, and it took me what seemed like forever to calm him down. He just didn't want me to leave him. I usually worked from home, but on occasion had to go into the office and drop him off at daycare, which he loved. But not on this particular morning. He didn't want day care, he didn't want his breakfast, he didn't want me to leave (he had seen my suitcase), and he didn't want me to touch him or talk to him. It was so frustrating. I had been packed for a couple of hours, and been busy with him for that period of time, just trying to get out of the house and on my way. I finally convinced him that I would bring him a nice new toy from the *'big city'* where I was going. He sniffled and finally relented. By the time we got out the door, I knew I would really need to hurry to catch my plane after dropping him off at day care.

And then traffic was moving so slow, I was sweating by the time I pulled into the airport parking. I grabbed my suitcase and my briefcase and ran. When I got to the gate, the plane had already taxied to the queue on the tarmac, waiting to take off. I could see it through the window, and watched it turn onto the runway and speed up. I had missed it. I was so disappointed, that I couldn't think of what I should do next. My schedule was so tight, that I would end up missing the beginning of the conference. There was no one at the gate desk to help me, so I had to go all the way back to the beginning where I had checked in. There wasn't another flight to my destination until that evening. What to do...what to do?? I decided that I should buy something for my son at the airport, and just go home. I decided that the conference just wasn't worth it. I would explain to my boss later that afternoon after I had enjoyed a relaxing glass of wine.

My boss was angry, but I figured that he would get over it. On the evening news that night, I found out that my son had actually saved my life. My flight had crashed and, although there were a few survivors who were injured, the part of the plane where I would have been sitting was where the people who died had been sitting. I would have died if I had made that plane. My whole family, except for my youngest, were all in shock, as was I. I spent that evening lying in bed with my young son reading a book to him as he held his new toy, just reveling in being with him. I couldn't even picture how it would have been for my family if I had been on that plane, especially this four-year-old little guy who always needed me near him. How horrible for my family. I was unable to get on a plane for several years after that. I felt that it was a warning to me, to stay home with my family and be safe.

We need to realize that things happen for a reason. And that is how I live my life now.

-   *From E. S. from Canada*

"Mom??"

*-When we lose people we love, sometimes they 'stick around'
to make sure all is well.-*

We knew she was dying from cancer. She held on to
see her granddaughter's wedding in the summer of 1998,
then passed away that December. I had been taking care of
her off and on for the past five years, enabling her to stay in
her beloved condo in South Carolina. Each time I visited, we
would review *"The List"*, which was who was to get what of
hers when she was gone. Thank heavens we had prepared the
list because she had a lot of things. And it made planning
much easier for my brother and myself when she died.

My brother and I spent about two weeks together in
her condo, packing and preparing two rental trucks that
would be used to get her belongings to our family.
Everything from furniture to jewelry was packed and tagged.
My brother was to drive his truck one way (enroute to his
home in the mid West) and mine for mostly down South

relatives on my way back home in Georgia.

My brother had left, and I was finishing cleaning up the condo which had already been sold. I was on the back patio, sweeping, and I looked up, back into the condo to the adjoining dining room. I saw a shadow of a woman on the wall, lighted by the dining room pendant light. That was funny, I thought to myself, I had locked the front door. I was certain. So, I went inside, saying *"Hello?"* I checked every room, plus the front door which was locked. No one. Then, I came back into the dining room, ready to pick up the broom on the back patio. I paused, wondering about what I had seen. And I felt someone or something touch my cheek. It felt cold on my warm skin. Then I felt coolness surround me, then let go. OK. I didn't see anyone, but I knew.

"Mom? I told you we would take care of everything. We followed your directions, and you will be happy to know that everything is packed and ready to go. And your condo sold in ten days. I know how much you loved it here. So, it's OK, you can go on. Everything is just fine here. I love you and I miss you, but you can go on now." And I waited, thinking I heard a faint sigh from *"her"*. Then nothing. She was gone.

I didn't start quivering until I went out to the truck, carrying my broom, ready to drop off the condo keys at a neighbors there. I felt a bit weird, hoping that it was indeed her and not *"something"* else. Then I headed on my way with a full truck, ready to stop by relatives and drop things off. I couldn't wait to get home.

The feelings I had that day have not faded. I know it was her. You see, she always wanted to rule everything and everyone, telling us all what to do and how to do it. So, I know her spirit was restless until she knew that I had taken care of everything. So typical of her.

- *From M. D. from Connecticut*

"The Strange Photos"

-We see this all the time on Facebook. And in magazines like 'People'. But why was this happening in her photos? –

You know how it goes. You have a family event, you take pictures...usually a lot of pictures. We have a large family, and that means really a LOT of pictures.

I recently was looking through some of my wedding and honeymoon. My mother had passed away a couple of years before, and I knew she had been there in spirit. She would have loved it, especially the dancing. She loved to dance.

In every photo, there was a fuzzy 'cloud' that was above our heads, not really much of a shape, but it was the SAME in every photo. It gave me goose bumps, and I just

• • •

couldn't figure it out. What was that?

When I looked at the pictures from our honeymoon, there it was again...in EVERY photo. I saw one where it was pretty clear to see, there was a white shape of 'someone' walking by the creek. I knew it, it was her!

I showed the pictures to my husband, and he just shrugged his shoulders. Soon after, I went to visit my father, and showed them to him. His face went so pale, I asked him if he was all right. Then, he looked at me and smiled, with the color coming back into his cheeks.

"Why, it's your mother. She wanted you to know that her spirit was with you." Was that it? Was it her?

Today, several years later, I look at those photos, and see how the wispy shape is there in all of them. Some were in the exact same location, looking the same. Sort of like steam or a cloud, hovering over us, most times over my shoulder, above my head. And the one by the creek, the one showing an actual body shape? Yes, I guess he is right. It must be my mother. Because I can feel her presence every time I look at them.

- *From T.D. from Georgia*

"A Spiritual Encounter"

-Sometimes things happen when we least expect them. –

This may not be as much of a ghost story, as it is more of a spiritual experience. I was a young adult just starting in a new profession in the Healing Arts. It was 2003 and I had much to learn.

I was working in a small salon at my first job, as an esthetician (skin care specialist). It was there that I met a woman in a bookstore adjacent to the salon. I developed a relationship with her and appreciated her wisdom. We will call her Nancy/

One day, I went in to grab a cup of tea during a break. *"Hi Nancy"*, I said. And she responded, *"Hi back. I've been meaning to ask you...have you ever heard of Reiki? There's a great book I just got in and it made me think of you.*

• • •

You're always eager to learn."

I answered, *"You know, just last week I was looking into what Reiki was."* Nancy suggested that I come back after I'm done at work and she will give me a session.

After work that day, I went into Nancy's store, where she had set up a massage table, dim lighting and ambiance, as if one were coming in for a facial service. She greeted me, *"Hi, I know you've been reading a little about Reiki, but how much do you know?"* Since I really didn't know much then, she suggested *"Lie down on the table. You're about to learn."* She continued, *"Reiki works by balancing the body and mind. We have energy centers in our body called Chakras, and they assist us with promoting full and whole body healing."*

My curiosity piqued, I was excited to begin. Nancy began by laying her hands on my head. Immediately, I began to feel a warmth, and a sense of peace. She placed her hands in different areas around my body. For the first time in a while, I felt a sense of peace.

"Nancy, where would I possibly learn something like this?" I asked her. She responded *"I thought you might want to know more about this. There's a woman I know in Old Lyme. Here's her number. Give her a call and see when her next class is."* I thanked her and left feeling so good.

The next morning, I gave the gal in Old Lyme a call. She promptly answered, *"Your timing's incredible. I have a class starting in two Saturdays from now. Are you interested?"* I was anxious to start, so I said *"Yes."*

I really looked forward to taking the class. I read the Reiki book to receive a fuller understanding. The Thursday before the class, I received a message from my mother, *"Please give me a call. It's important."*

When I called her, she shared with me the bad news, *"I need to tell you that your cousin Eric passed away. Can you come to Florida with me, as I need to go to your aunt's."*

At that time, having just started my new job, I was apprehensive about doing so. My other aunt chose to go with my mother instead of me.

I was saddened by the news, as Eric was just seventeen, and had his whole life ahead of him. He was an incredible fisherman, and the creatures of the water would always seem drawn to him. It was so tragic. I continued to work the next day, looking forward to the Reiki class on Saturday. Little did I know that something amazing was about to happen.

As I went into the Reiki class, the teacher began with an explanation of Reiki and the principles behind it. The first half of the class was a dive into what translates to *"life force."*

The second half of the class, we began a deep meditation, the intention being to begin the attunement of Reiki, basically the ability to offer a Reiki treatment to someone. *"I want you to become very comfortable in your seat, taking a few deep breaths,"* she said. She began ringing a few chimes, and the meditation began.

A couple of minutes in, I began to become a bit restless. I thought to myself, *"Is this worth it? What is this really about?"* As our teacher continued to speak, for whatever reason, I could feel the tension slipping from me. And I could feel myself beginning to deeply meditate. Entranced, I began to see the color of amethyst all around me. As I began to go deeper into the mediation, I saw a woman who appeared to be my grandmother, my mother's mother, who passed tragically in 1968, nine years before I was born.

"Hello, Sweetie. I've come to meet you. There's much I need to tell you and we only have a short time. I am you and you are me. I had more to do on Earth; I wasn't finished yet and came back...as you." The grandmother I never knew or rarely thought about, not having had known her, continued, *"Please tell your Aunt that I am taking care of Eric right now. He is with me, he is safe, though a little confused. But he is not afraid. I'm going to be watching over him for a while."*

"As for your mother, please tell her that what happened was not her fault. I do not have much time, but I'm paying attention to her. You have much to do in life, as 'we' are not done yet. There will be much more to happen. When someone crosses over, there is no pain, there is ease, there is a feeling of comfort. Eric will be OK, please let your aunt know. He is meant to be with me right now."

"There is so much more to say, but we must part for now. But know that I will be back to visit you in different times in your life. I also want you to know you can ask for me to come, even though you do not know me. I love you."

I became aware of my physical surroundings with the ding of a chime, and a soothing voice. I've never been able to explain that experience from nearly twenty years ago, but I know that it was a message I needed to hear from beyond.

\- *From H.P. in Connecticut*

"The Doubter"

-This one helped someone who was skeptical, understand what others have witnessed. –

Again, we have two stories here together. And this one is at the same time that was when we rented the house on Jameson Street in Ireland (my other story in this book). My second husband was such a doubter about the numerous times that myself and my sisters would see or feel spirits/ghosts.

Well, this one day, my sisters. cousin and I were sitting around the table talking about how my cousin had gotten a used long couch from a friend. Her friend had gotten it used from the Irish style store like Good Will called "Oxfam".

So, we were getting ready for a lot of family that was

going to come together to visit, wondering how we could provide room for everyone. My son and I were supposed to stay at this cousin's house. She had gotten the couch the night before we talked, and told me that she couldn't use the couch, because *"there was a man that came with it. He was lying on the couch and wouldn't move."* She couldn't even sit on it to watch television. Because of all the family that was coming, I had planned to spend that night with her, but surely wasn't going to with a man in her house that wouldn't leave *"his"* couch. My cousin wanted her friend to come back for the couch. Her friend didn't know who he was, but that is why she gave away the couch, as she couldn't use it either.

Naturally, my cousin didn't want the couch, and I certainly wasn't going into her house with that man there, so we needed to find someone to come and take the couch (and the man too). We tried once to move the couch, to maybe drag it out ourselves, but the man sat up and looked around, like *"What's happening here?"* We had dropped it and run out. We never did find out who he was or where he and his couch had come from. But a few days later, we did find someone to come and take the couch away. And she took her other couch back. She never told anyone else about the man on his couch. We figure that he must have died on that couch and went everywhere with it.

We had to finish talking about our stories, and go to the grocery store, but to go to Mom's house first to see what she wanted for supper. I left my husband there alone in the house. We were going to meet up later at Mom's house for supper.

We were on the way back from the store and saw my husband running down the street to my Mom's house. He looked so pale, acting strange.

Once inside, he told us his story. He started by saying, *"I will never doubt you ever again."* Then he proceeded to tell us that *"there was a wee woman and I sat on her lap!"* Apparently, after we had left him alone at the house, he was going to sit on the big comfy chair and stopped because a lady was sitting there. She had appeared suddenly, and he jumped over to the other chair. The lady just sat there, staring at him, not saying anything. (As he was telling us, it was really obvious that this whole experience shook him, as he was swearing, and spouting the story so that his false teeth almost fell out.)

Anyway, he didn't know what to do, but was so scared by her that he needed to go to the bathroom. He actually had spoken to her, saying *"Excuse me."* And then raced out of the house. And even now, he still had to go to the bathroom. Apparently, it was some lady that had died in that house.

He was no longer a doubter, as she had *"scared the shit out of me."*

-     *From P.S. in Connecticut*

"What's Up, George?"

-He just couldn't stay away. –

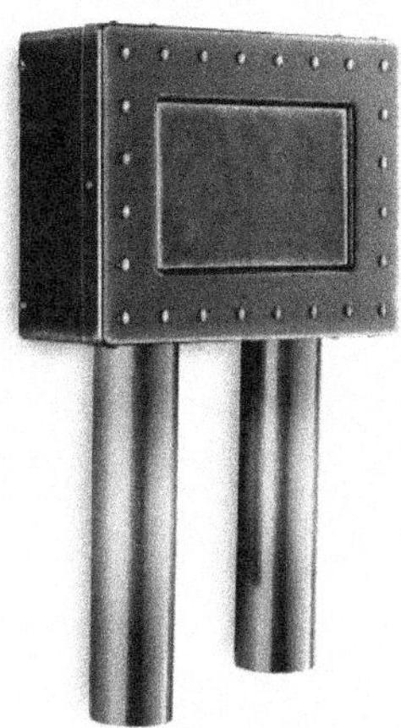

This was the most lingering spirit ever in my life. I call him George, because of our first experience with him. We moved into a house in Florida. My husband was in bed, we had a little dog named *"Coco"*, and I was sitting watching a movie relaxing. I was relaxing on the sectional, and Coco was on his dog bed. Then, suddenly, he came over and sat below our doorbell on the wall, staring and growling.

Now, that doorbell didn't work. We had disconnected it because of that. And we planned to remove it when we painted the wall in the near future. So, anyway, I couldn't figure out what was wrong with the dog. Then, I looked at the doorbell, which had a cloth covering on the box, and a couple of *"chime pendulums"* hanging down from it. That cloth covering was moving in and out, like it was breathing in and out! That scared me! I grabbed Coco and held him, and he kept growling. All the while, the cloth kept '*breathing*'.

I tried to wake up my husband. He was sleeping like a rock, so I couldn't do that. So, I came back into the living room, sat down, and suddenly, the cloth began *"breathing"* faster. I got mad, because it was bothering me, and I growled, *"For Christ's sake, what do you want?"* And it stopped moving. I went back to the movie, and then the doorbell began loudly dinging. And it kept dinging…

I couldn't believe it, that bell wasn't connected anymore, it was broken, there was no one outside pushing the doorbell (I looked), *"What was going on??!!"* That doorbell went on for maybe ten minutes. I ran into the bathroom to get away from it. It finally stopped dinging, so I came back out. All was quiet and my husband was still sleeping soundly, as was my son. So, I sat back down to watch the TV. The dog still went to that spot and still growled.

I watched probably for a half hour. Suddenly, 'wham, wham, wham'. Someone was banging on the windows. I thought it was maybe kids from the street. So, I beat on my husband to wake him up. By that time, the banging was done. So, he took a flashlight and went out to go around the house looking for anyone. There was no one.

He didn't believe me, telling me that I must have been dreaming. But then, my son came out and asked, *"What is all the noise, who was banging?"* Aha, someone else had heard it. It wasn't just me. They went back to bed, and I sat back down to finish the movie on TV.

Then, the TV shut off, as did all the lights in the living room. The lights in the bathroom and the kitchen were still on, but not where I was. Apparently, someone didn't want me to see that movie! So, I gave up and took the dog and went to bed, because Coco would have kept growling.

The next day, a friend of my son's came to the house, and I was telling her about it. She went to the courthouse and looked at the records of who lived and/or died there. A man named George did die there. So, now I knew who he was.

But he wasn't done with me. Every once in a while, things in the house would move. Spoons would go flying, even right out of the pot spraying gravy/sauce all over. No one was near it each time it happened. Everyone there saw it one time when spaghetti sauce was splashed all over as the ladle went flying. So, our expression was always *"What's going on, George?"* or *"George is at it again"*.

Every once in a while, something would happen, like the lights flipping on and off. And I would ask him, *"George, are you trying to tell me something?"* Quite often, something was happening that he wanted to warn me of, like the time when the lights were doing their *"George thing"*, and then someone came to the door knocking. One time it was one of my son's friends, who had just had a car accident.

George has followed us from place to place. So, every time, wherever we are, that something looks like George *'doing his thing'*, I ask *"What's up George?"*

-   *From P.S. in Connecticut*

"The Old Man in the Park"

-A walk through a park. And seeing someone that perhaps wasn't supposed to be there? –

I love to go for walks in the park. It is located between my apartment and my office, and no matter the season, it gives me great pleasure to walk through nature every day.

A few months ago, I began to notice an old man, sitting on one of the benches. No one else seemed to take notice of him, just me. As I walked by him, he smiled and took off his hat and sat it beside him. His clothes looked quite tattered, old and dirty, styles from the 1950s or 1960s. His hat was an old fedora, and he had a raincoat that was folded neatly beside him. On rainy days he would wear it. He looked like he could have been some kind of detective in his day, like he could be a picture from an old crime book or magazine.

I figured he might be around 60 or so, with gray hair

fringed around a bald head. His eyes would have a far away look in them, as if he was thinking of something long gone.

He looked so out of place there, that I was surprised that no one else seemed to see him or at least pay any attention to him. He never seemed to eat, just would sit there deep in thought. Except for the quick smile, nod of his head, and tipping of his hat (or taking it off) in recognition of seeing a lady. How I loved those old chivalrous ways men used to be decades ago.

One day, I decided to sit down next to him with my lunch and talk. He seemed quiet at first, but then said *"Hello"* in a deep, scratchy voice. He kept clearing his throat as if he hadn't talked in quite a while.

He said he had been a detective back in the early 1950s, and had lost his life there in the park, saving a 'damsel in distress'. I didn't quite know what to say to that, thinking that perhaps he was suffering some cognition loss. But he kept sharing with me. His story was that he was looking for someone to tell his story to, then he could finally rest, as no one had heard it yet. So, I listened quietly to him share his tale.

"She was in trouble, a man was hitting her, knocking her down, yelling at her. Turns out he was her husband, which he was quick to tell me. He told me that she was under his control, and it wasn't anybody else's business. Because I was a gentleman, I pulled him off her and slugged him. I told him I was arresting him for beating up a lady, and he took out a gun and shot me. Just like that!"

He seemed a bit upset about it and needed to clear his throat again. *"Well, I fell down, of course, and he dragged her off, probably to somewhere private so he could continue to hit her. She was crying. I tried to get up, but I was losing blood and consciousness fast, and didn't even have enough strength to pull out my own gun from my inside pocket."*

He looked so sad then. He looked down at the ground, sighed and finished with, *"Well, that was it. I couldn't help her. I couldn't even help myself. I guess they found me eventually, not knowing who shot me, or why."*

Then he looked up at me, *"My name is Sam Davis. Would you do me the courtesy of letting the police know what happened to me? I don't think my wife is alive anymore, so you don't need to tell her. We didn't have any children, so that would be the end of it. I just want it to go on record with what happened to me."*

I was feeling really strange, sitting there talking to what had proved to be a *'ghost'*. People who passed us apparently only saw me talking to myself, and walked away with funny looks, shaking their heads. But, to me, he was real. And I wanted to help him if I could.

"I would be happy to let them know. I will go there this afternoon, since I know the precinct is close by. When did this happen, so I can tell them?"

"It happened on April 1st, 1952, right over there by that big tree. April Fools on me, right?" He smiled at me sheepishly. So, I laughed with him.

Then he rose and grabbed his coat and hat and began to walk away. As I watched him, he gradually faded away. I guess he was finally '*at rest*', knowing he had done something good and would be known for it. I gathered my things and left for the police precinct. It was the least I could do.

- *From S.T. from Chicago*

"I'm Okay, Dad"

-Once again, she was visited by a loved one who wanted to make sure she was all right.-

I grew up very close with my father. I didn't meet him until I was almost two years old, as he had been away at France in WWII. So, I didn't know him when he came home and I cried when he tried to hug me. But it didn't take long for him to fill my heart, and I adored him, as he did me.

He had been sick for a couple of years, and I visited him and Mom as often as I could. I was pregnant and had my first child, a son, and was happy to bring the baby with me each time. He had been in renal failure for most of that time, and we all did the tests to see if anyone was a match to donate a kidney. But the specialists told us it was too late, as his heart wasn't strong enough for the surgery. So, he was on hemodialysis for most of that final year of his life. It broke my heart.

My husband, son and I visited him at the hospital during a weekend in that June, with my 16-month-old son, who loved to run around from person to person clapping his hands saying "*Hi*". My father was feeling better and was able to come out into the waiting room to see him and visit with us. How he laughed at my boy, who put on quite a show. I was so sad to leave and drive back the 80 miles, which felt too far away. Because we had plans that day (Sunday), we left before noon. Later in the afternoon, I had a bad feeling. It grew as the day grew later, and I decided to ask my girlfriend next door to watch my son that next morning, Monday, so I could drive back down to see Dad. I just knew I had to go. So, I did.

By the time I got there, Dad had fallen into a coma, and it wasn't expected that he would wake up. We began calling relatives to get as many there so they could at least hold his hand to say goodbye, especially my brother who was living with his family in another state. I held it together as long as I could, but when my brother and I went in to say our goodbyes and I felt my Dad faintly squeeze my hand, I kissed his forehead and flew from the room. I ran thru the waiting room and found a phone booth around the corner. I pulled the door closed in the booth, and I just fell apart. I couldn't stop and was still wailing when my husband found me. I still feel the pain and loss today, almost 50 years later.

You see, my mom and I weren't that close in life, but my Dad always understood me. It was like he could read my mind. It was a very special relationship. He passed away a few hours later. My heart was broken.

By the time we had his funeral and burial a few days later, I needed to sleep and let the pain overtake me. It was several hours later, and dark outside. I opened my eyes, and there at the foot of the bed was my Dad, just standing there looking at me with a sad look on his face. It was as if I could sit up and reach out my hand and touch him. He WAS there. So, I talked to him, *"Oh, Dad, my heart is broken. I miss you so much!"* Then tears just flooding my face. He looked at me, smiled and said, *"It's OK, sweetie. I will always be here for you. Just whisper my name and I will come to you. You may not be able to see me, but you will be able to feel me right beside you. I need to leave now, but I wanted to see you first. Just know that I will always love you."* Another sad smile, then he disappeared. I could see him very slowly fade from my sight, almost like he was reluctant to go.

And it was true, there were many times over those next decades that I needed to talk to him. And I felt him there, could even feet his hand on my shoulder sometimes. And a warmth would flow through me, and it would comfort me. I will never forget seeing him that night. It was REAL. And his voice was REAL.

- *From M.D. From Connecticut*

"Watching Over the Baby"

- Another story of someone else watching over us. –

When we lived in Yonkers, there was a *'spirit'* that visited us. We had moved there, my first husband and I and our new son. The crib was in our bedroom, which was our custom, at the base of our bed. We had a small window above our bed.

When the baby was about two months old, sleeping through the night, I woke up thinking I had heard the baby. I woke up and there was a light that came through the window over across the room to the crib. And I saw a man standing with his hand on the crib, looking on the baby. He was standing a little sideways. I couldn't see his face, but I saw that he was dressed in a long cloak like a monk would wear, brown with a rope around the waist. And he had the hood on, so all I could see was some of his gray hair but not his face. I thought he looked quite a bit like my dad, who lived in Ireland.

We were supposed to go to Ireland in a couple of

months, as we did every year to visit our family, and introduce our new son to his grandparents. The man just stood there, then moved his other hand up to the crib as if he was going to touch the baby. I watched this until the light went out, and he disappeared. The next day, I got a phone call that my cousin had died at just about that same time. We had all been very close, and we were looking forward to going home to see him. But he was the only one that I could think of as being the one who appeared in our home that night.

Was he giving us a message? Was he saying hello and goodbye to my son, whom he was supposed to meet but didn't? And shortly afterwards, one of our other sons became very ill, and perhaps it was a warning to watch over our sons? It's hard to tell, but we definitely had a visitor that night who wanted to "*meet*" our newest son.

-    *From P.S. in Connecticut*

"Her Cell Phone Selfies"

- She didn't remember taking these selfies. Why were they there in her phone's photos? –

Okay, this will be short because it's really weird. What does it mean when I find pictures of myself on my cell phone that I don't remember taking?? They look like selfies, but I didn't do them. I have tried to delete them, because it is just so weird. But then new ones appear. Who is this and why are they teasing me like this?

I got so weirded out that I got rid of that phone and bought a new one, even a different brand. And guess what? More selfies of myself appeared. What the heck? I am in my early 20's, am a responsible human being, with a good job, and am very self-sufficient. This is just too weird. What do you think?

I even went to my church and asked my priest, who

said he could do a blessing on my phone in case it was the '*work of the devil*'. Something else to add to my weird list.

And, actually, it did stop. But I feel like I am waiting for it to happen again, because I just don't understand it. And yes, you can include this in your new book, as long as you do as you promise, keep me anonymous. I don't want people to feel I am strange, you know?

- *From T. C. from Louisiana*

"Seeing The Future"

-   He could see the future and write about it. But they didn't believe him. They should have known better. –

When I worked in a publishing house, I heard about this obscure writer that would send in stories that were foretellings, that would then actually happen within the year. This was when I lived and worked in London. I did get to read a couple of the stories, I guess you would call them novelettes today, short novels. But they were based on events that did happen, just months after we would receive the stories.

I didn't get to meet that particular author, I was just a copy editor, but I heard about him. Apparently, he had been born with a thin layer of skin over his face, called a caul or veil, and he proved to be able to know things way ahead of time. I researched and found that when a baby is born with this, it is actually a piece of amniotic sac still attached to the face. It is pretty rare and is a sign of good luck usually. But in this instance, it gave him a *'second sight'*.

For instance, he would know whether a baby would be

a boy or a girl, about a war that would happen, stating the exact year way ahead of time, about who would be assassinated in office and when and where, and the list goes on. I have heard that when someone is born with this '*condition*', they can see things with like a sixth sense or something.

This particular person who saw himself as an unpublished author (because we didn't publish his work and would send it back to him with a rejection letter), developed a reputation of being correct 100% of the time when people approached him to find things out about the future. He never charged, I understand, but felt that his gift should be shared. But to me, it is entirely creepy.

One of his stories was about the Kennedy assassination, with dates and places, and this was written 20 years ahead of time. He didn't name President Kennedy but called him a '*young politician from Massachusetts who would be the first Catholic president, who came from a large wealthy family and who would die in Dallas, Texas.*' And he stated the date and circumstances, that it would happen in a parade of cars with open tops. He also wrote about the Vietnamese War, with details in another story. I mean, it was crazy, but would always prove correct each and every time.

Keep in mind that these stories were written about 20 years or 25 years before they would happen. I just can't handle this kind of thing. But, thank you for allowing me to share this with you. It haunts me to this day. I hope that actually writing about it will help me not to have nightmares about it. It is just too weird.

- *From S. H. in England*

NOTE FROM THE EDITOR:

My personal experience similar to this story included my maternal great-grandmother who was also born with a caul or veil. She could foretell many things too, such as whether someone would be having a boy or girl, as well as the Kennedy assassination, and World War II, as well as the Vietnam War, and so many other things. Since she passed away when I was a pre-teen, I know this mostly from my family members. I wonder how many other people have been born this way and had this ability? - *MWD*

"My First Encounter"

- When you are young, it can be VERY confusing when you have an encounter with a spirit. –

When I was about ten, I had my first '*ghost encounter*'. There was a time, living in Ireland, when we had a small house and there were several of us sleeping in this big bed, and being the '*runt*', I slept against the wall. One night, I had to get up and go to the bathroom, which was downstairs and outside. I got up and saw this little lady kneeling by the window in our room, praying, looking out the window, with her rosary in her hands. Scared, I quickly got back in bed to hide and covered up my head with my blanket. She was a little lady, with a white hat, dark dress and white pinafore apron on her, like a maid. It took me peeking out three times before she was finally gone. It was around 5:30 in the morning by then.

I went downstairs and told my father what had happened, as he was stoking the fire to warm us all up. His response was that I was dreaming and to talk to my mother about it. Well, my mother was a real doubter, and told me I was dreaming too. I knew I wasn't. Three days later after the scene kept repeating itself, I went to school and told my teacher about it. She was very religious. I told her that the little lady did me no harm, but it scared me, as I was so young and didn't know what was going on. She told me just to say a prayer for the lady, who was probably a lost soul that had lost her way.

That night, my parents went to the movies, and my brother and I were alone in the house. I wanted to go and get some candy. It was raining, I had my hood up and when I went to the pedestrian crossing, it was difficult to see. When I began to cross, I was hit by a white van. I was afraid to tell my mom because my school uniform sleeve was stuck in the cut on my arm, and I had hit my head. The man who drove the van was very shook up. And this neighbor girl saw me and wanted to take me home. But the driver wanted to take me home himself to make sure I was ok. Then I went inside and went to bed. I couldn't get my sweater off because of the cut.

The next day I went to school, putting my school uniform dress on over the sweater. When I went home, my mother was there to meet me, which was unusual. She had heard about the accident and wondered why I hadn't told her. I told her I was afraid. Later I found out the next day that the man in the white van came to our house to see if I was ok. He turned out to be the boyfriend of the girl three doors up. My mother took me up the street the next day, to the girlfriend's house. My mother introduced me to her, as she had been talking with this girl about my dream visions. Well, this gal took a picture out of her pocket of her mother, and I told her that was the little lady I saw every night in my bedroom. It turned out that her mother used to live in that house, and that was her bedroom where she had died. She had been a maid. So that explained who the praying little maid was. After I saw the picture, I never saw her again.

- *From P.S. in Connecticut*

"She Looks Just Like Me"

- I have heard that everyone has a 'doppelganger'. But when she saw 'hers', it wasn't what she expected.-

My parents have always thought I had too much imagination. They are both college professors, as are my two brothers. But as the only girl, they figured that I was probably just too spoiled, allowed to do my *'own thing'*. They tried to be patient with me, but seemed to be separate emotionally and physically, finding it difficult to *'deal with me'*. Not that I was a problem child, but I just had quite a wild imagination.

When I decided to study journalism at a NYC college, I was fortunate enough to live with my aunt in her apartment only a few blocks from the college. My aunt was quite the character, somewhere between a hippie and an 'artiste', another family member that my parents and brothers had difficulty relating to. Apparently, when my parents were younger and my brothers were little, they had lived in the same apartment building as my aunt. They moved shortly after my birth to CT, where they found jobs in a college there. And that's where we grew up.

Gradually, over a short period of time, I began to notice that when I looked in the mirror, there was a sort of hazy spot behind me that I could see in the mirror, but not when I turned around to look for it. I didn't think too much about it at first, but the haze began to form into what looked like a young girl. And over a short period of time, her face began to form, and...she looked just like me! I asked my aunt about it, and she just threw up her hands, and said *"The Lord only knows. Strange things happen in this building."* And walked away.

I really needed to know what was going on. Especially when one day I saw her walking on the street! She looked just like me, but dressed in very plain clothes, a long dress and long coat. She looked almost like she was floating rather than walking. I decided to follow her. I didn't care if I would be late for class, this was too important. I needed an answer. She turned a corner, and I ran to catch up. I wanted to meet her and talk with her and ask her who she was. But when I turned the corner, she had disappeared. Completely, no trace.

I was due to visit home for a couple of weeks on school break soon and decided to talk with my parents about it. I wasn't looking forward to it, as I was sure they would just say, *"Another strange case of imagination with our daughter."* But they didn't say that. What they said blew my mind.

My mother turned very pale when I told her about the mirror image and the girl on the street that looked just like me. She turned to my father, who looked shocked. Then tears fell down my mother's cheeks. *"Oh, honey, it must be your sister."* Then a lot more tears. Then she told me the story. *"When we lived in NYC, you and your twin sister were born. You looked identical as babies, but she had a heart problem, something to do with one of her heart valves. So she only lived a few weeks. It broke our hearts."*

Wait, I had a twin sister?? And she was haunting me? Was it because I was there in that apartment building where we had lived when she died? Part of me didn't want to know. It just creeped me out. I may have an active imagination, but this was too much.

Soon after, I transferred to a college in CT, had my aunt ship my things, and didn't return back to NYC. I may, somewhere inside, miss having my sister, but not as a ghost. That just wasn't ok. I never talked about it again and tried not to think about it. But, seeing as I can tell about it in this book without being identified, I decided *"Why not?"*

And, yes, it is all true. I have not been back to NYC since, and just can't. I don't want to see her. I know you might think, *"Why not? Aren't you curious?"* No, I am not curious enough to do that. It has been over 50 years, and I just couldn't ever do it. Call me a scaredy cat or a fool. Would you go back to try to see her? That is the stuff, to me, that is found in nightmares. Not for me.

-   *From S. J. from Connecticut*

"Go Away!!"

*- Was it all a dream? She was so afraid,
that it had to be real .-*

I woke up with a feeling like I was still half inside my dream and half-awake in the here and now. I felt like I had traveled elsewhere and left a part of me there. I struggled to wake up and looking around seeing shadows of people. I couldn't see more than just the shadowy shapes against the coming light of a new day. I was alone in the bed and the room, no current husband there, after suffering thru a hard divorce. I felt scared. What was happening?

It felt like several people had broken into my home and were watching me sleep.

I was shaking, and fell back onto my pillow and pulled the covers up and over my head, like a scared child.

"Go away!" was the only thing I could utter out of my tight-lipped mouth. Every muscle in my body was tight, almost like a full body *'charley horse.'*

I could feel them moving closer to the bed...closer to me. I felt so scared, wondering who they were.

"Who are you?" No response. And even though I was so scared, I wondered if perhaps I might still be asleep and dreaming this. It was so quiet all I could hear was my fast breathing and feel my heart trying to jump out of my chest. Curiosity overcame everything else and I peeked over my covers to take a look, hoping they were gone.

They were still there like inky blobs in human shapes close to the end of my bed. Suddenly the shapes began to disperse as if they were melting, slowly becoming dark clouds and then were gone, as if a breeze blew them away.

What was happening? I felt so chilled even though my covers were thick. It took me several moments before my body settled back down to normal. But my brain wouldn't stop questioning, '*was it all a dream?*' I got out of bed to get some water, then settled back under the covers.

Okay, did I remember the dream? Vaguely, I remembered that in the dream it was a family gathering and we were all talking and laughing, my grandparents, my aunts and uncles, my patents. They were all there and in the dream I felt surrounded by love.

Now as I recalled how the dream felt, I realized that the shadows hadn't acted threatening. Since I was no longer as emotional but more logical, I realized that it could have been one of two things. Either they were still a part of my dream that carried thru into my semi-awakening grogginess, or they were representing some of my family trying to show me they were still watching over me.

How will I know for sure? I guess I never will. It is up to me how I feel about it, and I choose to think it was a part of my dream state, and as I woke up, they dispersed, just like the dream did. Gone but not forgotten. Never forgotten. Even today as I remember this after 30 years, I can still feel the quick fear, followed by the confusion of just what the heck happened.

-   *From C.G. from New York*

"The Television Remote Went Weird"

- She couldn't believe it kept happening. The TV channels kept changing all by themselves .-

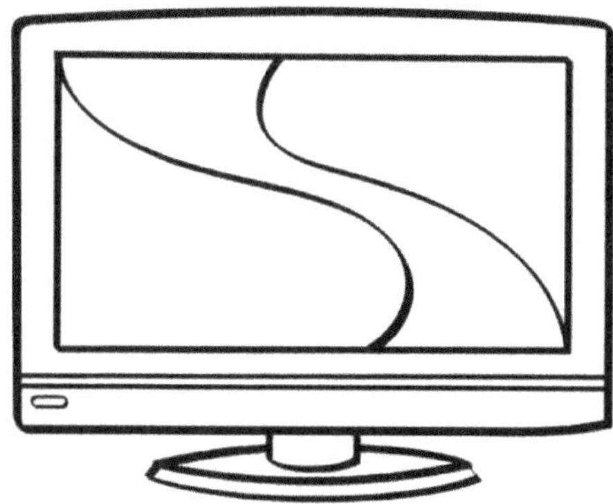

This was something that happened to my family quite regularly but was very weird. We live in a very nice neighborhood in the suburbs and are quite friendly with some of our neighbors. We have children who play with one another, and we are involved in our neighborhood schools and community. In the evening, when we settle down to watch some television and relax, we don't want to think about work or life outside our home. It is a time of peaceful and calm relaxation for my husband and me. The kids are in their rooms either studying or asleep. This is 'our' time.

Well, for the longest time, every once in a while, we would be watching a show, and then the station would change to another program. Without us touching the remote. So, we would then change it back to our show so we could continue to watch. On occasion, the volume would also change, and we would need to reset it to our comfort level. There were a few times when the channels would start flipping through, and we couldn't stop it until it settled onto one show. Then, at last, we would have the control back in order to change it to our preferred program. It was so frustrating. We had no idea what was going on.

Our teenage daughter, who has a very open mind, told us it was probably a ghost. Well, that didn't set well with us older adults who work in the scientific field and simply don't believe in such things.

One day, we were talking with our next-door neighbor and told him about it. And he laughed, saying to us that it happened to him too. When we compared the types of remotes we use, we figured it out. It was our neighbor changing our channels. And it was us changing his. How weird is that? But to us, it made perfect sense. A lot better than a ghost, isn't it? Go technology.

Actually, this happened to us many years ago, and it doesn't happen anymore. Our neighbor now has a Dish and we use Cable. We each have control now over our own televisions. Less frustrating. So, this is one '*ghost story*' that actually has a rational explanation. And it is the closest to one that we have, I hope you don't mind our sharing it here. You need to have at least one story that is rational.

-   *From C. T. from Massachusetts*

NOTE FROM THE EDITOR:

This is funny to me, as the same thing has happened off and on to us through the year. Now that I know that it was technology instead of TV remote 'ghosts', I am quite relieved. - *MWD*

● ● ●

ABOUT THE AUTHOR

Marilyn Wright Dayton has been writing all of her life, from the time she could hold a pencil. Her life and career focused on the world of advertising in many roles. She was one of the originators of some of the more unique marketing vehicles in the nation over the years.

As an innovator in the new world of women and leadership, she has proven to create peak performances in startups, small business and non-profits. From the beginning of her career at the age of 12 as a radio quiz kid, she has been both in front of the camera and behind the camera as a fashion model, radio and TV show host and program producer. She holds degrees in marketing and business as well as in journalism. Over the past several decades, she has also been a newspaper reporter, creative writer, ad director, entrepreneur, a consultant, a trainer and an authority in the areas of creative marketing and top-notch business performance.

Through those years, her first loves have continued to be creative writing and art. She brings that to her other books, "*Beyond*", "*Reflexions*", and "*Our Roots Run Deep*" which is an historical perspective on her family genealogy. Upcoming will be five murder mysteries based on the four 70-ish women who live in a nursing home but love to solve mysteries, who were first introduced in "*Beyond*".

Marilyn is now retired from the business world and makes her home with her family in Mystic, CT.

Beyond 2